50 Lost Cookbook of Atlantis Recipes

By: Kelly Johnson

Table of Contents

- Trident's Golden Seafood Stew
- Oceanic Herb-Crusted Salmon
- Poseidon's Grilled Lobster Tails
- Sunken Treasure Shellfish Paella
- Seafoam Coconut Shrimp Curry
- Sapphire Tuna Tartare
- Deep-Sea Lemon Butter Scallops
- Atlantean Honey-Glazed Swordfish
- Coral Reef Crab Cakes
- Pearl Diver's Clam Chowder
- Ancient Spiced Octopus Grill
- Neptune's Roasted Garlic Mussels
- Mystical Seaweed and Citrus Salad
- Golden Seabream with Herbal Infusion
- Atlantis-Style Pomegranate Glazed Duck
- Ocean Mist Oysters Rockefeller
- Emerald Isle Stuffed Calamari
- Sunken Garden Avocado Shrimp Salad
- Mariner's Saffron Infused Rice
- Lost City Lemon Thyme Halibut
- Celestial Starfruit and Lobster Ceviche
- Deep Current Blackened Red Snapper
- Undersea Herb Butter Prawns
- Mythical Honey-Crusted Barramundi
- Seafarer's Pineapple-Ginger Glazed Tuna
- Moonlit Mango and Chili Crab
- Hidden Gem Citrus-Rosemary Seabass
- Sapphire Bay Poached Salmon with Dill
- Nautical Nectar Caramelized Scallops
- Sunken Treasure Roasted Squid with Garlic
- Ocean's Bounty Baked Clams with Parmesan
- Atlantean Citrus and Basil Shrimp Skewers
- Sea Sorcerer's Saffron Broth with Mussels
- Golden Coast Fire-Roasted Snapper
- Mystical Blueberry and Lime Glazed Cod

- Twilight Tidal Wave Tuna Poke Bowl
- Enchanted Bay Thyme and Lemon Crab Legs
- Ancient Harvest Roasted Fennel and Fish
- Ocean Depths Spiced Tuna Carpaccio
- Hidden Lagoon Charred Lobster Medallions
- Atlantean Silk Coconut Cream Clam Soup
- Poseidon's Treasure Chest Smoked Trout
- Serene Shores Garlic-Lime Grilled Oysters
- Deep Blue Mango Passion Glazed Mahi-Mahi
- Coral Blossom Gingered Scallops
- Ocean Whisper Tamarind and Honey Shrimp
- Atlantis Glow Fire-Seared Octopus
- Lost Relic Pineapple-Soy Marinated Fish
- Azure Tide Lemon Butter Crab Bisque
- Eternal Ocean Vanilla-Citrus Poached Pears

Trident's Golden Seafood Stew

Ingredients:

- 1 lb mixed seafood (shrimp, mussels, clams, squid)
- 2 tbsp olive oil
- 1 onion, diced
- 3 garlic cloves, minced
- 1 cup white wine
- 4 cups seafood broth
- 1 can (14 oz) diced tomatoes
- 1 tsp saffron threads
- ½ tsp smoked paprika
- ½ tsp salt
- ½ tsp black pepper
- ½ cup chopped parsley

Instructions:

1. Heat olive oil in a large pot and sauté onions and garlic until translucent.
2. Pour in wine and simmer for 3 minutes.
3. Add broth, tomatoes, saffron, paprika, salt, and pepper. Simmer for 10 minutes.
4. Add seafood and cook for 5 minutes until shellfish opens.
5. Garnish with parsley and serve hot.

Oceanic Herb-Crusted Salmon

Ingredients:

- 4 salmon fillets
- ½ cup panko breadcrumbs
- ¼ cup chopped parsley
- 2 tbsp fresh dill
- 1 tbsp lemon zest
- 2 tbsp olive oil
- ½ tsp salt
- ½ tsp black pepper

Instructions:

1. Preheat oven to 400°F (200°C).
2. Mix panko, parsley, dill, lemon zest, olive oil, salt, and pepper.
3. Press the mixture onto salmon fillets.
4. Bake for 12-15 minutes until golden.

Poseidon's Grilled Lobster Tails

Ingredients:

- 4 lobster tails
- 4 tbsp butter, melted
- 2 garlic cloves, minced
- 1 tbsp lemon juice
- ½ tsp paprika
- ½ tsp salt
- ½ tsp black pepper

Instructions:

1. Preheat grill to medium-high heat.
2. Split lobster tails and brush with a mixture of butter, garlic, lemon juice, paprika, salt, and pepper.
3. Grill for 5-7 minutes until meat is opaque.

Sunken Treasure Shellfish Paella

Ingredients:

- 1 ½ cups Arborio rice
- 1 tbsp olive oil
- 1 onion, diced
- 3 garlic cloves, minced
- ½ cup white wine
- 4 cups seafood broth
- 1 tsp saffron
- ½ lb shrimp
- ½ lb mussels
- ½ lb clams
- ½ cup peas
- 1 tsp smoked paprika
- ½ tsp salt
- Lemon wedges for garnish

Instructions:

1. Heat oil in a pan and sauté onion and garlic.
2. Add rice and stir for 1 minute.
3. Pour in wine, then broth, saffron, paprika, and salt.
4. Simmer for 15 minutes, then add shellfish and peas.
5. Cover and cook for another 10 minutes until shellfish opens.
6. Serve with lemon wedges.

Seafoam Coconut Shrimp Curry

Ingredients:

- 1 lb shrimp, peeled and deveined
- 1 can (14 oz) coconut milk
- 2 tbsp red curry paste
- 1 tbsp fish sauce
- 1 tbsp lime juice
- 1 red bell pepper, sliced
- ½ cup chopped cilantro
- 2 tbsp olive oil

Instructions:

1. Heat oil in a pan and sauté curry paste for 1 minute.
2. Add coconut milk, fish sauce, and lime juice.
3. Simmer for 5 minutes, then add shrimp and bell pepper.
4. Cook until shrimp is pink. Garnish with cilantro.

Sapphire Tuna Tartare

Ingredients:

- ½ lb fresh sushi-grade tuna, diced
- 1 tbsp soy sauce
- 1 tsp sesame oil
- 1 tsp lime juice
- ½ tsp grated ginger
- 1 tbsp chopped chives
- 1 tbsp diced avocado

Instructions:

1. Mix all ingredients in a bowl.
2. Chill for 10 minutes before serving.

Deep-Sea Lemon Butter Scallops

Ingredients:

- 1 lb sea scallops
- 2 tbsp butter
- 1 tbsp olive oil
- 2 garlic cloves, minced
- 1 tbsp lemon juice
- ½ tsp salt
- ½ tsp black pepper

Instructions:

1. Heat oil in a pan over medium-high heat.
2. Sear scallops for 2 minutes per side.
3. Add butter, garlic, and lemon juice.
4. Serve hot.

Atlantean Honey-Glazed Swordfish

Ingredients:

- 4 swordfish steaks
- ¼ cup honey
- 2 tbsp soy sauce
- 1 tbsp lime juice
- 1 tsp grated ginger

Instructions:

1. Mix honey, soy sauce, lime juice, and ginger.
2. Marinate swordfish for 30 minutes.
3. Grill for 5 minutes per side.

Coral Reef Crab Cakes

Ingredients:

- 1 lb crab meat
- ½ cup panko breadcrumbs
- 1 egg
- 1 tbsp mayonnaise
- 1 tbsp Dijon mustard
- ½ tsp salt
- ½ tsp black pepper
- 2 tbsp olive oil

Instructions:

1. Mix all ingredients except oil.
2. Shape into patties and refrigerate for 30 minutes.
3. Heat oil and cook crab cakes for 3 minutes per side.

Pearl Diver's Clam Chowder

Ingredients:

- 1 lb clams
- 2 cups diced potatoes
- 1 onion, chopped
- 2 garlic cloves, minced
- 3 cups seafood broth
- 1 cup heavy cream
- 2 tbsp butter
- ½ tsp thyme
- ½ tsp salt

Instructions:

1. Melt butter in a pot and sauté onion and garlic.
2. Add potatoes, broth, thyme, and salt. Simmer for 15 minutes.
3. Add clams and cook until they open.
4. Stir in cream and serve.

Ancient Spiced Octopus Grill

Ingredients:

- 1 lb octopus, cleaned
- 2 tbsp olive oil
- 1 tsp smoked paprika
- 1 tsp ground cumin
- ½ tsp chili flakes
- 2 garlic cloves, minced
- 1 tbsp lemon juice
- Salt and black pepper to taste

Instructions:

1. Boil octopus in salted water for 45 minutes until tender. Drain and pat dry.
2. Mix olive oil, paprika, cumin, chili flakes, garlic, lemon juice, salt, and pepper.
3. Brush marinade onto octopus and let sit for 30 minutes.
4. Grill over medium-high heat for 3-4 minutes per side.

Neptune's Roasted Garlic Mussels

Ingredients:

- 2 lbs fresh mussels, cleaned
- 4 tbsp butter
- 4 garlic cloves, minced
- ½ cup white wine
- 1 tsp lemon zest
- ½ tsp salt
- ½ tsp black pepper
- Chopped parsley for garnish

Instructions:

1. Preheat oven to 375°F (190°C).
2. Melt butter and sauté garlic in a pan. Add wine, lemon zest, salt, and pepper.
3. Place mussels in a baking dish, pour sauce over, and bake for 10 minutes until mussels open.
4. Garnish with parsley and serve.

Mystical Seaweed and Citrus Salad

Ingredients:

- 1 cup dried seaweed, rehydrated
- 1 orange, segmented
- 1 grapefruit, segmented
- ½ cup sliced cucumbers
- 1 tbsp sesame oil
- 1 tbsp rice vinegar
- 1 tsp soy sauce
- 1 tsp honey
- 1 tsp toasted sesame seeds

Instructions:

1. Mix seaweed, orange, grapefruit, and cucumber in a bowl.
2. Whisk together sesame oil, rice vinegar, soy sauce, and honey.
3. Toss salad with dressing and sprinkle with sesame seeds.

Golden Seabream with Herbal Infusion

Ingredients:

- 2 whole seabream, cleaned
- 2 tbsp olive oil
- 1 tbsp lemon juice
- 1 tsp fresh thyme
- 1 tsp fresh rosemary
- 1 garlic clove, minced
- ½ tsp salt
- ½ tsp black pepper

Instructions:

1. Preheat oven to 400°F (200°C).
2. Stuff seabream with thyme, rosemary, and garlic.
3. Drizzle with olive oil and lemon juice, then season with salt and pepper.
4. Bake for 20-25 minutes until flaky.

Atlantis-Style Pomegranate Glazed Duck

Ingredients:

- 2 duck breasts
- ½ cup pomegranate juice
- 2 tbsp honey
- 1 tbsp balsamic vinegar
- ½ tsp cinnamon
- ½ tsp salt
- ½ tsp black pepper

Instructions:

1. Score duck skin and season with salt and pepper.
2. Sear skin-side down in a pan for 5 minutes, then flip and cook another 3 minutes.
3. Mix pomegranate juice, honey, balsamic vinegar, and cinnamon in a saucepan and reduce until syrupy.
4. Brush glaze over duck and roast at 375°F (190°C) for 10 minutes.

Ocean Mist Oysters Rockefeller

Ingredients:

- 12 fresh oysters, shucked
- 2 tbsp butter
- 2 garlic cloves, minced
- ½ cup spinach, chopped
- ¼ cup heavy cream
- ¼ cup Parmesan cheese
- ¼ cup panko breadcrumbs
- ½ tsp salt
- ½ tsp black pepper

Instructions:

1. Preheat oven to 400°F (200°C).
2. Sauté garlic and spinach in butter, then add cream, salt, and pepper. Simmer until thickened.
3. Spoon mixture over oysters and sprinkle with Parmesan and panko.
4. Bake for 10 minutes until golden.

Emerald Isle Stuffed Calamari

Ingredients:

- 6 large squid tubes, cleaned
- ½ cup cooked rice
- ¼ cup feta cheese, crumbled
- ¼ cup chopped spinach
- 1 garlic clove, minced
- ½ tsp oregano
- ½ tsp salt
- ½ tsp black pepper

Instructions:

1. Mix rice, feta, spinach, garlic, oregano, salt, and pepper.
2. Stuff squid tubes and secure with toothpicks.
3. Grill over medium heat for 3-4 minutes per side.

Sunken Garden Avocado Shrimp Salad

Ingredients:

- 1 lb cooked shrimp
- 1 avocado, diced
- 1 cup cherry tomatoes, halved
- ½ cucumber, diced
- 2 tbsp olive oil
- 1 tbsp lime juice
- ½ tsp salt
- ½ tsp black pepper

Instructions:

1. Mix shrimp, avocado, tomatoes, and cucumber in a bowl.
2. Whisk together olive oil, lime juice, salt, and pepper.
3. Toss salad with dressing.

Mariner's Saffron Infused Rice

Ingredients:

- 1 cup Arborio rice
- 2 cups seafood broth
- 1 tsp saffron threads
- 1 tbsp butter
- ½ tsp salt
- ½ tsp black pepper

Instructions:

1. Heat butter in a pan and add rice, stirring for 1 minute.
2. Add saffron and broth, then simmer for 15-20 minutes.
3. Season with salt and pepper.

Lost City Lemon Thyme Halibut

Ingredients:

- 2 halibut fillets
- 2 tbsp olive oil
- 1 tbsp lemon juice
- 1 tsp fresh thyme
- ½ tsp salt
- ½ tsp black pepper

Instructions:

1. Preheat oven to 375°F (190°C).
2. Mix olive oil, lemon juice, thyme, salt, and pepper.
3. Brush onto halibut and bake for 15 minutes.

Celestial Starfruit and Lobster Ceviche

Ingredients:

- 1 lb cooked lobster meat, chopped
- 1 starfruit, thinly sliced
- ½ red onion, finely diced
- 1 jalapeño, minced
- ½ cup fresh lime juice
- 2 tbsp fresh orange juice
- 1 tbsp olive oil
- ¼ cup chopped cilantro
- Salt and black pepper to taste

Instructions:

1. Combine lobster, starfruit, red onion, and jalapeño in a bowl.
2. Pour lime juice, orange juice, and olive oil over the mixture.
3. Season with salt and pepper, then mix well.
4. Let marinate for 20 minutes, then garnish with cilantro before serving.

Deep Current Blackened Red Snapper

Ingredients:

- 2 red snapper fillets
- 1 tbsp olive oil
- 1 tsp smoked paprika
- 1 tsp cayenne pepper
- 1 tsp garlic powder
- ½ tsp salt
- ½ tsp black pepper
- 1 tbsp butter

Instructions:

1. Rub snapper fillets with olive oil and season with spices.
2. Heat butter in a skillet over high heat.
3. Sear snapper for 3-4 minutes per side until blackened and crispy.

Undersea Herb Butter Prawns

Ingredients:

- 1 lb large prawns, peeled and deveined
- 3 tbsp butter
- 2 garlic cloves, minced
- 1 tbsp lemon juice
- 1 tsp fresh parsley, chopped
- ½ tsp salt
- ½ tsp black pepper

Instructions:

1. Melt butter in a pan and sauté garlic for 1 minute.
2. Add prawns and cook for 2-3 minutes per side.
3. Stir in lemon juice, parsley, salt, and pepper.

Mythical Honey-Crusted Barramundi

Ingredients:

- 2 barramundi fillets
- 2 tbsp honey
- 1 tbsp Dijon mustard
- ½ cup panko breadcrumbs
- 1 tbsp olive oil
- ½ tsp salt
- ½ tsp black pepper

Instructions:

1. Preheat oven to 400°F (200°C).
2. Mix honey and mustard, then brush over fish.
3. Coat fillets with panko, salt, and pepper.
4. Drizzle with olive oil and bake for 15 minutes.

Seafarer's Pineapple-Ginger Glazed Tuna

Ingredients:

- 2 tuna steaks
- ½ cup pineapple juice
- 1 tbsp grated ginger
- 1 tbsp soy sauce
- 1 tbsp honey
- ½ tsp black pepper

Instructions:

1. Whisk pineapple juice, ginger, soy sauce, and honey.
2. Marinate tuna for 30 minutes.
3. Sear over medium-high heat for 2-3 minutes per side.

Moonlit Mango and Chili Crab

Ingredients:

- 1 lb cooked crab meat
- 1 ripe mango, diced
- 1 red chili, minced
- 1 tbsp lime juice
- 1 tbsp honey
- ½ tsp salt
- ½ tsp black pepper

Instructions:

1. Mix crab meat, mango, chili, lime juice, honey, salt, and pepper.
2. Serve chilled or at room temperature.

Hidden Gem Citrus-Rosemary Seabass

Ingredients:

- 2 seabass fillets
- 2 tbsp olive oil
- 1 tbsp lemon juice
- 1 tsp fresh rosemary, chopped
- ½ tsp salt
- ½ tsp black pepper

Instructions:

1. Preheat oven to 375°F (190°C).
2. Mix olive oil, lemon juice, rosemary, salt, and pepper.
3. Brush onto fish and bake for 15-18 minutes.

Sapphire Bay Poached Salmon with Dill

Ingredients:

- 2 salmon fillets
- 2 cups vegetable broth
- 1 tbsp white wine vinegar
- 1 tsp fresh dill, chopped
- ½ tsp salt
- ½ tsp black pepper

Instructions:

1. Heat broth and vinegar in a pan until simmering.
2. Add salmon and poach for 10 minutes.
3. Garnish with dill before serving.

Nautical Nectar Caramelized Scallops

Ingredients:

- 1 lb scallops
- 2 tbsp butter
- 1 tbsp honey
- ½ tsp salt
- ½ tsp black pepper

Instructions:

1. Heat butter in a pan over high heat.
2. Sear scallops for 2 minutes per side.
3. Drizzle with honey and cook for 1 more minute.

Sunken Treasure Roasted Squid with Garlic

Ingredients:

- 1 lb squid, cleaned and cut into rings
- 2 tbsp olive oil
- 2 garlic cloves, minced
- ½ tsp salt
- ½ tsp black pepper
- ½ tsp paprika

Instructions:

1. Preheat oven to 400°F (200°C).
2. Toss squid with olive oil, garlic, salt, pepper, and paprika.
3. Roast for 10-12 minutes.

Ocean's Bounty Baked Clams with Parmesan

Ingredients:

- 12 fresh clams, scrubbed
- ¼ cup unsalted butter, melted
- ¼ cup grated Parmesan cheese
- 2 garlic cloves, minced
- 1 tbsp fresh parsley, chopped
- ½ tsp lemon zest
- ½ tsp black pepper
- ¼ cup breadcrumbs

Instructions:

1. Preheat oven to 375°F (190°C).
2. Open clams and place them on a baking sheet.
3. Mix butter, garlic, parsley, lemon zest, and black pepper.
4. Spoon mixture onto each clam and top with Parmesan and breadcrumbs.
5. Bake for 10-12 minutes until golden brown.

Atlantean Citrus and Basil Shrimp Skewers

Ingredients:

- 1 lb large shrimp, peeled and deveined
- 2 tbsp olive oil
- Juice of 1 orange
- Juice of 1 lemon
- 1 tbsp honey
- 2 tbsp fresh basil, chopped
- ½ tsp salt
- ½ tsp black pepper
- Wooden skewers, soaked

Instructions:

1. In a bowl, whisk olive oil, citrus juices, honey, basil, salt, and pepper.
2. Marinate shrimp for 20 minutes.
3. Thread shrimp onto skewers and grill for 2-3 minutes per side.

Sea Sorcerer's Saffron Broth with Mussels

Ingredients:

- 2 lbs fresh mussels, cleaned
- 2 tbsp olive oil
- 2 garlic cloves, minced
- ½ cup white wine
- 2 cups seafood broth
- 1 pinch saffron threads
- ½ tsp salt
- ½ tsp black pepper
- 2 tbsp fresh parsley, chopped

Instructions:

1. Heat olive oil in a pot and sauté garlic for 1 minute.
2. Add white wine, seafood broth, saffron, salt, and pepper. Simmer for 5 minutes.
3. Add mussels, cover, and cook for 5-7 minutes until they open.
4. Garnish with parsley before serving.

Golden Coast Fire-Roasted Snapper

Ingredients:

- 1 whole red snapper, cleaned
- 2 tbsp olive oil
- 1 tbsp lemon juice
- 1 tsp smoked paprika
- ½ tsp salt
- ½ tsp black pepper

Instructions:

1. Preheat grill to medium-high heat.
2. Rub snapper with olive oil, lemon juice, paprika, salt, and pepper.
3. Grill for 5-7 minutes per side until flaky.

Mystical Blueberry and Lime Glazed Cod

Ingredients:

- 2 cod fillets
- ½ cup fresh blueberries
- Juice of 1 lime
- 1 tbsp honey
- 1 tsp fresh thyme
- ½ tsp salt
- ½ tsp black pepper

Instructions:

1. Blend blueberries, lime juice, honey, thyme, salt, and pepper into a glaze.
2. Brush over cod fillets and bake at 375°F (190°C) for 12-15 minutes.

Twilight Tidal Wave Tuna Poke Bowl

Ingredients:

- 1 lb fresh tuna, diced
- 2 tbsp soy sauce
- 1 tbsp sesame oil
- 1 tsp sriracha
- ½ tsp grated ginger
- 1 avocado, sliced
- ½ cup diced cucumber
- 1 cup cooked sushi rice
- 1 tsp sesame seeds

Instructions:

1. Mix tuna, soy sauce, sesame oil, sriracha, and ginger in a bowl.
2. Serve over rice with avocado and cucumber.
3. Garnish with sesame seeds.

Enchanted Bay Thyme and Lemon Crab Legs

Ingredients:

- 1 lb crab legs
- 3 tbsp butter, melted
- 1 tsp fresh thyme
- 1 tsp lemon juice
- ½ tsp salt
- ½ tsp black pepper

Instructions:

1. Steam crab legs for 5-7 minutes.
2. Mix butter, thyme, lemon juice, salt, and pepper.
3. Brush over crab legs before serving.

Ancient Harvest Roasted Fennel and Fish

Ingredients:

- 2 white fish fillets (halibut, cod, or seabass)
- 1 fennel bulb, sliced
- 2 tbsp olive oil
- 1 tsp lemon zest
- ½ tsp salt
- ½ tsp black pepper

Instructions:

1. Preheat oven to 375°F (190°C).
2. Toss fennel with olive oil, salt, and pepper, then spread on a baking sheet.
3. Place fish fillets on top, sprinkle with lemon zest, and roast for 15 minutes.

Ocean Depths Spiced Tuna Carpaccio

Ingredients:

- 1 lb fresh tuna, thinly sliced
- 2 tbsp olive oil
- 1 tbsp soy sauce
- ½ tsp chili flakes
- ½ tsp black pepper
- 1 tsp sesame seeds
- 1 tsp lime juice

Instructions:

1. Arrange tuna slices on a plate.
2. Drizzle with olive oil, soy sauce, and lime juice.
3. Sprinkle chili flakes, black pepper, and sesame seeds.

Hidden Lagoon Charred Lobster Medallions

Ingredients:

- 2 lobster tails, cut into medallions
- 2 tbsp butter
- 1 tsp smoked paprika
- ½ tsp salt
- ½ tsp black pepper
- 1 tbsp lemon juice

Instructions:

1. Heat butter in a skillet over high heat.
2. Sear lobster medallions for 2 minutes per side.
3. Sprinkle with paprika, salt, and pepper, then finish with lemon juice.

Atlantean Silk Coconut Cream Clam Soup

Ingredients:

- 1 lb fresh clams, scrubbed
- 1 can (14 oz) coconut milk
- 2 cups seafood broth
- 1 tbsp butter
- 2 garlic cloves, minced
- 1 small onion, finely chopped
- 1 tsp grated ginger
- ½ tsp turmeric
- ½ tsp salt
- ½ tsp black pepper
- 1 tbsp fresh cilantro, chopped

Instructions:

1. In a pot, melt butter over medium heat. Sauté garlic, onion, and ginger until fragrant.
2. Add turmeric, salt, and pepper. Stir in seafood broth and coconut milk. Bring to a simmer.
3. Add clams, cover, and cook for 5-7 minutes until clams open.
4. Garnish with fresh cilantro and serve hot.

Poseidon's Treasure Chest Smoked Trout

Ingredients:

- 2 whole trout, cleaned
- 2 tbsp olive oil
- 1 tbsp sea salt
- 1 tsp black pepper
- 1 tsp smoked paprika
- 1 lemon, sliced
- Wood chips for smoking

Instructions:

1. Preheat smoker to 225°F (107°C) and soak wood chips.
2. Rub trout with olive oil, salt, pepper, and paprika.
3. Stuff lemon slices inside the fish cavity.
4. Smoke for 1.5-2 hours until flaky.

Serene Shores Garlic-Lime Grilled Oysters

Ingredients:

- 12 fresh oysters, shucked
- 2 tbsp butter, melted
- 2 garlic cloves, minced
- 1 tbsp lime juice
- ½ tsp salt
- ½ tsp black pepper

Instructions:

1. Preheat grill to medium-high heat.
2. Mix butter, garlic, lime juice, salt, and pepper.
3. Place oysters on the grill, spoon the mixture over each, and grill for 2-3 minutes.

Deep Blue Mango Passion Glazed Mahi-Mahi

Ingredients:

- 2 mahi-mahi fillets
- ½ cup mango puree
- 2 tbsp passion fruit juice
- 1 tbsp honey
- ½ tsp salt
- ½ tsp black pepper

Instructions:

1. Mix mango puree, passion fruit juice, honey, salt, and pepper.
2. Brush over fillets and bake at 375°F (190°C) for 12-15 minutes.

Coral Blossom Gingered Scallops

Ingredients:

- 1 lb scallops
- 2 tbsp butter
- 1 tbsp grated ginger
- 1 tsp soy sauce
- ½ tsp salt
- ½ tsp black pepper

Instructions:

1. Heat butter in a pan over medium-high heat.
2. Sear scallops for 2 minutes per side.
3. Add ginger, soy sauce, salt, and pepper. Sauté for another minute.

Ocean Whisper Tamarind and Honey Shrimp

Ingredients:

- 1 lb shrimp, peeled and deveined
- 2 tbsp tamarind paste
- 1 tbsp honey
- 1 tbsp soy sauce
- ½ tsp chili flakes

Instructions:

1. Mix tamarind, honey, soy sauce, and chili flakes.
2. Marinate shrimp for 20 minutes.
3. Sauté in a pan over medium heat for 3-4 minutes per side.

Atlantis Glow Fire-Seared Octopus

Ingredients:

- 1 lb octopus, cooked and cut into pieces
- 2 tbsp olive oil
- 1 tsp smoked paprika
- ½ tsp salt
- ½ tsp black pepper

Instructions:

1. Heat a pan over high heat with olive oil.
2. Sear octopus for 2-3 minutes per side until charred.
3. Sprinkle with paprika, salt, and pepper.

Lost Relic Pineapple-Soy Marinated Fish

Ingredients:

- 2 white fish fillets
- ½ cup pineapple juice
- 2 tbsp soy sauce
- 1 tsp grated ginger

Instructions:

1. Marinate fish for 30 minutes.
2. Grill for 4-5 minutes per side.

Azure Tide Lemon Butter Crab Bisque

Ingredients:

- 1 lb crab meat
- 2 tbsp butter
- 2 cups seafood broth
- 1 cup heavy cream
- 1 tsp lemon zest
- ½ tsp salt
- ½ tsp black pepper

Instructions:

1. Sauté crab meat in butter.
2. Add broth, cream, lemon zest, salt, and pepper.
3. Simmer for 10 minutes before serving.

Eternal Ocean Vanilla-Citrus Poached Pears

Ingredients:

- 2 pears, peeled and halved
- 2 cups water
- 1 vanilla bean
- 1 orange, juiced
- ¼ cup honey

Instructions:

1. Simmer water, vanilla, orange juice, and honey in a pot.
2. Add pears and poach for 15 minutes.

www.ingramcontent.com/pod-product-compliance
Lightning Source LLC
LaVergne TN
LVHW061955070526
838199LV00060B/4137